# PEACEFUL PLAYGROUNDS

### AN ELEMENTARY TEACHER'S GUIDE

### TO

### RECESS GAMES AND MARKINGS

by

MELINDA BOSSENMEYER

**EDITOR**
Frank Alexander

**COVER DESIGN/TEXT COUPONS & AWARD**
Dawn Bates

**TEXT DIAGRAMS**
Loren Jenks

Published by FRONT ROW EXPERIENCE, 540 Discovery Bay Blvd., Byron, CA 94514

Published

by

FRONT ROW EXPERIENCE
540 Discovery Bay Blvd.
Byron, California 94514

**NOTICE**
The information in this book is true and complete to the best of our knowledge.
It is offered with no guarantees on the part of the author or Front Row Experience.
The author and publisher disclaim all liability in connection with use of this book.

# DEDICATION

This book is dedicated to Barbara Austin who first proposed the "peace on the playground" concept. Many of the games listed in this guide were first recorded by Mrs. Austin.

Mrs. Austin was an elementary school Physical Education teacher in the Oakland Unified School District, Oakland, California. Her contribution to California school children continues with the teaching of peaceful playground concepts.

\* A special thanks to Pat Bledsoe for her valued input on safety considerations. Pat is a consultant and teacher for the ABC Unified School District, Cerritos, California.

# ABOUT THE AUTHOR

Melinda Bossenmeyer, M.S., is a public school educator. She is the mother of two children. She is the owner and director of Kinder/Kids Gym, a children's motor development program in Southern California. Her other credits include:

*   Consultant for California State Department of Education

*   Teacher Trainer for Elementary School Physical Education

*   Master's Degree in Physical Education

*   Mentor Teacher for the Alvord School District, Riverside, CA

*   Author of Perceptual-Motor Development Guide; Front Row Experience, Byron, CA

# CONTENTS

# INTRODUCTION

How would you like your playground to be a peaceful place for fun and games?

How would you like your students to be actively involved in purposeful play?

How would you like to never have to solve another playground argument?

Sound impossible? It's not! The key to a peaceful playground lies within the following five principles:

1)   All students must be taught a consistent set of rules.

2)   Students need a procedure for handling conflicts and must be taught how to do this without adult intervention.

3)   Game markings must be painted on the playground.

4)   The necessary equipment must be available.

5)   Consistent expectations from school personnel must be enforced.

# RULE#1: CONSISTENT SET OF RULES

A consistent set of rules must be distributed to all staff members and playground supervisors at the beginning of the school year. A staff inservice is important for implementing success. After the first year, a short meeting is suggested to review and make changes to rules which have presented problems during the first year. (Remember, the rules that each school follows may be altered to meet the needs of each school site.) The important concept which should be emphasized is that each member of a school's staff should instruct his/her students in A CONSISTENT SET OF RULES.

An effective method of teaching children the various rules and activities contained within this book is to introduce "a game-a-day" during the allotted physical education class time. Game rules can be posted on the Game Bulletin Board so that students have the opportunity to review rules as needed.

# RULE#2: SOLUTIONS TO CONFLICTS

Appropriate social interaction must be taught so that students have the tools for handling their playground problems and disagreements.

A tool for children to utilize in solving their playground conflicts is called an Emergency Plan*. The Emergency Plan most often used is called Rock, Scissors, Paper. Children play this game when they have a disagreement. For example, if two students are pushing and shoving and both insist that they are the first in line then they should play Rock, Scissors, Paper. Likewise, if two students are arguing as to who is out in tether ball, then they use the Emergency Plan to settle the argument as well.

Guiding Principles:

1) Both children make a fist and use a pounding motion on their available hand simultaneously. On the third pounding motion, each child selects either rock, scissors or paper. In the case of a tie—repeat the procedure.

2) A rock will break scissors.

3) Paper will cover a rock.

4) Scissors will cut paper.

The Emergency Plan works in solving most all playground conflicts.

An alternative to the Emergency Plan is to use the first three students waiting in line to referee the game. The responsibility of the referees is to: 1) Stop Play; 2) Site The Infraction; and 3) Rule Accordingly.

*Emergency Plan concept was first introduced by Rudy Benton a P.E. specialist from Oakland Unified School District in Oakland, California.

# RULE#3: GAME MARKINGS

It goes without saying that if the markings for a particular game are not painted on the blacktop or "burned" into a field then it is very difficult to enforce consistent rules. School district maintenance personnel can be called upon to complete this task. Most respond if enough information is provided. The EXACT measurements for each game will be required. (See Appendix for additional suggestions in this area.) As well, they need a master plan of your playground in order that they may position the games in the correct spot on your playground.

Each game contained within this book lists the appropriate measurements and markings for each activity. A safety line or restraining line has been included when necessary. You may wish to alter the measurements in order to fit the space available on your playground.

Finally, the "out-of-sight-out-of-mind" principle surely applies here. If the game is painted on the blacktop or burned into the field, then students are reminded visually each time they pass by. Whereas, if the student has recently learned a new game or activity, he or she may soon forget it without the visual reminder.

To distinguish safety lines from other markings, a different color such as red paint should be used. Note that this type of a safety precaution may come from the district budget instead of the school site budget as most districts allow for this provision.

The two best methods of permanent markings are:

#### Grass
Lines are sprayed with weed killer. This is known as "burning in" lines. This method is best and lasts between 3-6 months. It is suggested that all lines be resprayed every four months to prevent the need to remeasure. A lime marker can be used on grass also. This method of "chalking" lines lasts only 3-6 days.

#### Blacktop
Painting lines on the blacktop is the most permanent and time efficient method. Chalking the blacktop is a temporary solution that should be followed up by permanent painting.

# RULE#4: NECESSARY EQUIPMENT AVAILABLE

Most educators agree that books, paper and pencils are critical equipment to successful academic instruction. The playground too, requires appropriate equipment for successful game participation. If students are required to share text books, then the classroom teacher observes immediate breakdown in active participation and discipline problems may arise. So too, is the case of the playground. If equipment must be shared, then this means that the number of actively or directly involved students is reduced. This in turn, as in the academic setting, is conducive to a discipline situation.

A central check-out system with one individual in charge of checking out and retrieving all equipment is generally far superior to the conventional method of distributing equipment to each classroom. The central check-out person should have students sign out for a piece of equipment so that he or she may track down a missing or unreturned piece of equipment at the end of recess (see Appendix 5). This also allows for one person to monitor the maintenance and care of equipment so that equipment is properly inflated and children will not spend half of the recess chasing around trying to track down someone with a ball pump to reinflate a flat ball.

Marking school equipment with the school name is highly suggested.

*Note: The "Lifetime" of a ball is one year, therefore, the annual budget should reflect yearly replacement costs.

# RULE#5: CONSISTENT EXPECTATIONS

It is important that not only each class follow a consistent set of rules but also that each teacher and school staff member require that students handle conflicts using the procedures outlined in Rule #2.

If a staff member settles conflicts for students, this soon leads to the students believing that their role in handling conflicts is limited or nonexistent.

It is suggested that students be reminded of their role and responsibility in this process and encouraged to use the Emergency Plan. A gentle reminder is usually all that is necessary.

---

# A, MY NAME IS...

### GOOD FOR
Hand-eye coordination, motor planning, sequencing of letters and initial letter practice.

### OBJECT
To successfully complete the rhyme while executing the correct motor movements.

### EQUIPMENT
Ball

PROCEDURE

1) Player bounces ball repeating the following rhyme:

   A, my name is_____
   (girl's name beginning with A)

   And my husband's name is_____
   (boy's name beginning with A)

   We come from_____
   (place beginning with A)

   And we sell_____
   (product beginning with A)

2) The rhyme is repeated for every letter in the alphabet. Each time the player mentions one of the letter words, she must pass her leg over the ball.

3) A player misses when she or he loses the ball, fails to pass leg over, or fails to insert an appropriate word in the rhyme. When child misses, the next child takes a turn.

4) Start where you missed when your turn comes again.

# AROUND THE WORLD

## GOOD FOR
Hand-eye coordination, basketball shooting practice and number sequencing.

## OBJECT
To successfully make baskets at spots 1-8.

## EQUIPMENT
Basketball (kickball or yellow utility ball will do), basket, and chalk to mark numbers (better yet, paint the numbers).

## PROCEDURE

1) The numbers 1-8 are marked on the ground within the throwing distance of the basket. All children in the game line up behind the number 1. Have them note carefully their place in the line.

2) First child tries to throw the ball into the basket. If successful, he moves to the number two and shoots again. He continues to shoot from successively higher numbers until he misses.

3) When he misses, the next child in line has his turn. Each child starts at one and tries to put the ball into the basket from each number. When he misses, he stays at the number which he missed and awaits his next turn.

4) The first child to complete all the numbers is the winner. If you do not have a basket, or wish to play indoors, use a box and a slightly deflated ball.

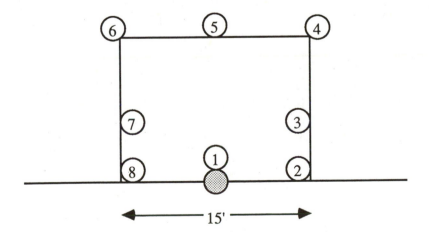

# BACK UP

## GOOD FOR
Hand-eye coordination.

## OBJECT
To successfully complete actions on lines 1-6 in order.

## EQUIPMENT
Ball, wall, and lines numbered consecutively from wall.

### PROCEDURE

1)  Child stands behind line number one and throws ball to wall. She allows it to bounce one time and catches it while standing in position behind line number one.

2)  If she succeeds, she repeats the action from line two allowing one bounce. She continues to back up to the next line until she misses. When she misses, the next child takes her turn. When the first player has another turn, she begins at the line at which she missed.

3)  When a player has thrown and caught successfully from the last line, she starts again from line one but may not allow the ball to bounce before catching it.

4)  Missing the ball, having the wrong number of bounces, stepping over the line or catching and throwing from the wrong number are misses.

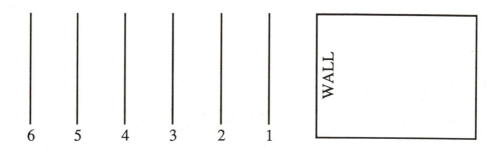

# BALL HOP SCOTCH

### GOOD FOR
Hand-eye coordination, eye-foot coordination and sequencing of numbers.

### OBJECT
To successfully bounce ball in each square the correct number of times in order.

### EQUIPMENT
Half of a sixteen square court and a ball that can be bounced.

PROCEDURE

1) Player stands outside of the court opposite box number one.

2) He rolls the ball into box number one and runs after it. He must stop the ball while his two feet are in the box.

3) He bounces the ball one time in the box. Then he steps, in order, from each box number 1-8 and bounces the ball one time in each box. He may not step on any lines while he moves from one box to another.

4) When he finishes, he returns to the position outside of box number one and rolls the ball into box number two. He runs through box one into box two and catches the ball as before. He bounces the ball two times in box number two, then moves to box number three and continues to bounce the ball two times in boxes 2-8.

5) He then rolls the ball to box number three and does the same thing bouncing the ball three times in each box, numbers 3-8. He continues in the action until he misses, at which point it is the next child's turn. When his turn comes again, he begins in the box he missed.

6) The first player to finish the entire court is the winner.

Fouls or Misses are:

1) Failure to stop the ball with both feet in the correct box.

2) Bouncing the wrong number of times.

3) Stepping on a line.

4) Failure to run through every box up to the ball, that is, when the ball is rolled to box eight, the child must run through every box from 1-7 to get to box eight before the ball rolls out of box eight. He may not run directly to box eight.

| 4 | 5 |
|---|---|
| 3 | 6 |
| 2 | 7 |
| 1 | 8 |

2'

2'

# BASKETBALL

**GOOD FOR**
Hand-eye coordination.

**OBJECT**
To score points by shooting the ball into the basket.

**EQUIPMENT**
Basketball (size appropriate to age) and basketball court.

## PROCEDURE

1) There are five players on each basketball team.

2) Play begins at the center of a circle in the middle of the court with a jump ball.

3) After each successful basket the ball is put into play at the end of the court under the basket by the team against whom the score was made.

4) A basket from anywhere in the court scores two points. A free throw from the free throw line scores one point.

5) If the ball goes out-of-bounds, it is given to an opponent of the player who last touched the ball. It is thrown in from the point that it went out-of-bounds.

6) Any player on the team may shoot for a goal.

**Fouls:**

Fouls occur when a player trips, pushes, holds, charges, or has body contact with an opponent. A foul results in the opposition player fouled receiving a free throw from the free throw line.

**Violations:**

All violations result in the opposing team getting the ball from out-of-bounds.

1) Traveling—taking more than one step with the ball without passing, dribbling or shooting.

2) Stepping out-of-bounds with the ball or causing the ball to go out-of-bounds.

3) Taking more than 10 seconds to shoot a free throw.

4) Kicking the ball.

5) Stepping on or over a restraining line during a jump ball.

6) Remaining more than three seconds in the key when your team has the ball.

7) Double dribbling—dribbling with two hands or dribbling a second series of times without passing the ball.

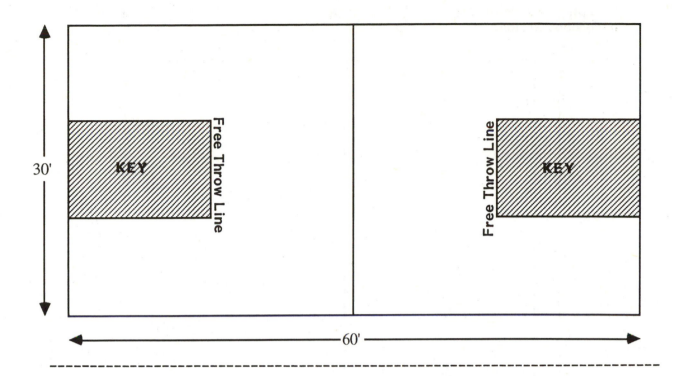

# BEAN BAG FOUR SQUARE

### GOOD FOR
Hand-eye coordination

### OBJECT
To get to square A and remain there by eliminating opponents in squares B-D
while not allowing bean bag to land in your square.

### EQUIPMENT
Four clorox scoops, one bean bag, and four square game markings.

PROCEDURE

1) The game is played like regular four square. Each of four children stand in one of the boxes. Extra children line up outside of box D. Child in box A starts the game by throwing the bean bag with her scoop to person in box D.

2) When a foul occurs, the child who fouls goes to the end of the line; the first child on the waiting line comes into box D, and the other children move up to fill any vacated squares.

Fouls:

1) Having the bean bag fall on the ground in your square, even if you are the thrower.

2) Throwing the bean bag so that it falls outside of the four square area or on a line.

3) Touching the bean bag with anything other than a scoop.

4) Dumping the bean bag out of the scoop. It must be thrown forward with an underhand action.

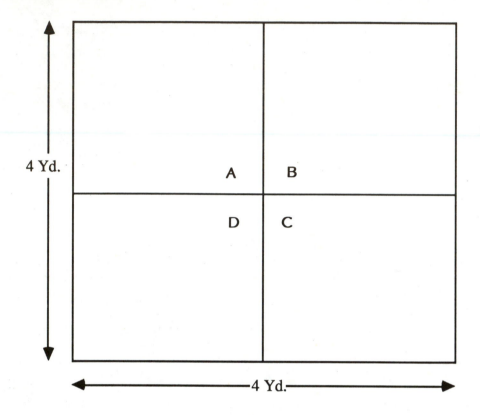

-------------------------------------------------------------------------

# BEAN BAG TOSS TARGET GAME

**GOOD FOR**
Hand-eye coordination, addition and counting by "fives" practice.

**OBJECT**
To throw bean bag into points area to score the greatest number of points.

**EQUIPMENT**
Bean bags and target area.

**PROCEDURE**

1) The game is played with two throwers. Each thrower stands behind the end line and throws the bean bag, alternating turns. Each player has two throws to attempt the highest number of points.

2) No points are awarded for a bean bag touching a line.

3) After each player has taken their two throws, the totals should be added to determine the winner. The next child in line would then challenge the winner.

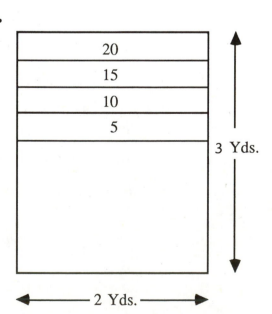

# BOUNCE BALL

### GOOD FOR
Hand-eye coordination.

### OBJECT
To score points by rolling or bouncing the ball across the opponents' end line.

### EQUIPMENT
One ball for each team and a rectangular playing area.

PROCEDURE

1)   A rectangular playing area is divided into two halves by a center line.

2)   Each team has a playground ball.  The object is to bounce or roll the ball over the opponent's end line.

3)   Players can move wherever they wish in their own area but may not cross the center line.

4)   Play begins and a point is scored for each ball crossing over the end line on a bounce or roll.


Fouls:
   Stepping over the center line.

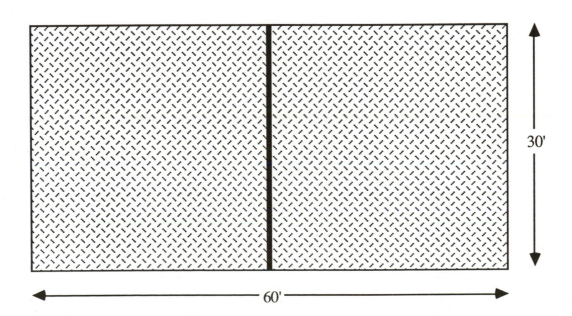

# CHINESE ROPES

**GOOD FOR**
Eye-foot coordination and sequencing of motor movements.

**OBJECT**
To successfully execute skills in progression without an error.

**EQUIPMENT**
Chinese jump rope (special elastic circular rope).

PROCEDURE

1) Two players (rope-holders) hold the Chinese jump rope by facing each other and placing the rope around the backs of their ankles. Their feet should be shouder-width apart and the rope should be fairly tightly stretched between them but not so much as to cause discomfort on the backs of their ankles.

2) The jumper stands on the outside of the rope loop beside the right or left side of the stretched rope near its middle facing one of the rope-holders. She touches her foot nearest the rope to the floor in the loop made by the rope and returns to her starting position. Repeat 4 times.

3) Jumper hooks same foot under the closer rope and lifts the rope across to the far side over the other farther rope and steps on this foot. Jumper then hooks other foot from inside (the space created by forcing one rope beyond the other) under the other formerly farthest rope and stands in stride position. When she does this, the jumper will now be standing with one rope pressed snugly against the left side of her left ankle and the other rope pressed snugly against her right ankle. She then jumps forcefully up releasing the rope(s) and lands in stride position without stepping on the rope(s).

4) If successful, do the same facing the rope; repeat facing opposite direction. If successful at this level, raise the rope higher on the legs and repeat.

------------------------------------------------------------------------

# CIRCLE STRADDLE BALL

**GOOD FOR**
Hand-eye coordination.

**OBJECT**
To roll ball between opponents' legs.

**EQUIPMENT**
Playground ball and circle court.

PROCEDURE

1) Children stand in a circle with a straddle position, feet touching feet of players on either side and hands on the knees.

2) One or two balls may be used depending on the skill and age of the students.

3) The object of the game is to roll the ball between the legs of another player before he can get his hands down to stop the ball.

4) Each time a ball goes between the legs of an individual, a point is scored.

5) The players with the fewest points scored against them are the winners.

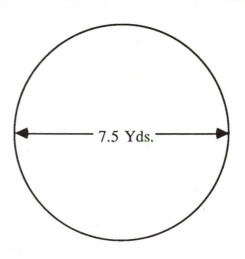

7.5 Yds.

---------------------------------------------------------------------------

# ELIMINATION DODGE BALL

### GOOD FOR
Body and space awareness, hand-eye coordination, eye-foot coordination and locomotor practice.

### OBJECT
To roll or throw ball at center player in order to become a "dodger".

### EQUIPMENT
Nerf ball or playground ball and circle court (see previous game above for dimensions).

## PROCEDURE

1) Players outside of the circle try to hit the player inside of the circle with the ball by throwing it rapidly. Hits must be recorded below the waist.

2) The player in the middle, to avoid being hit by the ball, may move, jump, and stoop but may not touch the ball.

3) Outside players may enter the circle to get the ball, but must throw the ball from outside of the circle. They may not carry the ball outside of the circle and give it to one of their friends.

4) Players number off in twos. Ball carrier names ones or twos to be first. The person that hits the inside circle player takes the place of the person that has been hit.

Fouls:

1) Catching the ball.

2) Stepping on or over the line with foot to throw the ball. Arm follow-through is OK.

3) No physical contact between players.

4) Hitting.

5) "No lives", no subs.

# FOUR SQUARE

## GOOD FOR
Hand-eye coordination.

## OBJECT
To get to square A and remain there by eliminating opponents in squares B-D.

## EQUIPMENT
Utility ball or a ten inch playground ball and Four Square game markings
(see top of page 10 for Four Square dimensions).

PROCEDURE

1) The squares are lettered A, B, C and D. The serve always starts from square A.

2) Players take positions in boxes A, B, C and D.

3) The ball is served by dropping it and serving it underhand from the bounce. If the serve hits a line, the server is out. To begin the game, the server hits the ball to square D.

4) The player receiving the ball must keep it in play by striking the ball after it has bounced once in his square. He may return the ball from outside of the perimeter. He directs it to another square with an underhand hit.

5) Play continues until one player fails to return a hit or commits a foul. When someone fouls, the first child at the waiting line enters at box D. All children then advance to fill in the available square.

Fouls:

1) Failure to hit a ball that bounces into one's box.

2) Playing a ball that has bounced into someone else's box.

3) Hitting the ball out of bounds or onto a line.

4) Hitting the ball into one's own box.

5) Holding the ball, catching or carrying a return volley.

# FREEZE OUT

### GOOD FOR
Hand-eye coordination.

### OBJECT
Cooperate with opponent by making good throws and catches in order to remain playing.

### . EQUIPMENT
Ball or bean bag or scoops and a bean bag, or a pair of socks—anything children can throw and catch, and two restraining lines 6 yards apart.

### PROCEDURE

1) Two active players line up behind either of two restraining lines facing each other.

2) The person on each line plays catch with the person across from him. These two children continue to throw back and forth until one misses.

3) When one child misses, BOTH children must go to the end of their lines and two new children step up to play.

4) The children do not try to put one another out, but try to play cooperatively as long as possible.

5) Distance and throwing rules (bounces or no bounces) can be established according to the ability of the children playing.

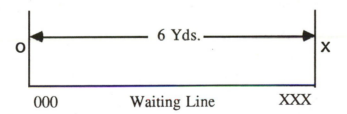

# HANDBALL

### GOOD FOR
Hand-eye coordination.

### OBJECT
To remain in play by successfully returning the ball to the wall.

### EQUIPMENT
Red utility ball or tennis ball and a handball court.

## PROCEDURE

1)   One service only.  Server must stand behind the service line.

2)   Server and opponent stand facing the wall.  All others wait their turn back out of the way.

3)   The server drops ball on the floor once and hits the ball, on the rebound, up to the wall.  The opponent may refuse one serve only.  The opponent may hit the ball on the fly or after it bounces once.

4)   Serve must be over the service line from the wall and ball must hit above 2 foot line on the wall.

5)   The server and opponent alternate hitting the ball to the wall until one player fails to hit the ball, fails to get the ball to hit the wall, or lets the ball bounce more than once, or commits a foul of some sort.  The ball may be hit with an open hand or with a closed fist.

Fouls:
   The server loses his serve (opponent becomes server) or opponent is out (opponent goes to end of wait line and new opponent comes in) when:

1)   Server steps over serving line.

2)   Any rebounding ball does not cross the 2 foot service line on the floor.

3)   Ball is thrown against the wall instead of using bounce or a hand stroke.

4)   Ball is caught or stopped.

5)   Server plays own serve.

6)   They fail to strike the ball following the first bounce.

7)   They fail to return the ball.

8)   Ball does not hit above the 2 foot line on the wall.

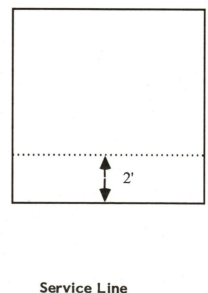

2'

2'

Service Line

9)    Ball hits any other object other than the wall.

10)    Ball goes out of bounds (if side lines or "out-of-bounds" lines are marked).

11)    Ball is hit twice in succession.

12)    Ball is juggled.

-----------------------------------------------------------------------

# HIT THE STICK

### GOOD FOR
Hand-eye coordination.

### OBJECT
To return ball by bouncing it on the stick.

### EQUIPMENT
Ball, stick (preferably one that won't roll such as a popsicle stick)
and a playing field as illustrated below.

## PROCEDURE

1)    Two players face each other.  One stands behind the Winner Line and the other behind the Challenger Line.  A Wait Line is formed for remaining challengers.

2)    Halfway between the two players a line is drawn and a stick is placed on it. The children bounce a ball back and forth between them trying to hit the stick.

3)    The child who first moves the stick is the winner and stands behind the Winner Line.  The loser goes to the end of the Wait Line and a new child becomes the challenger.  The challenger always throws first.

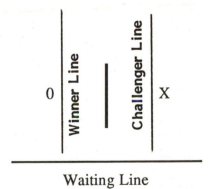

Waiting Line

# HOME RUN

### GOOD FOR
Eye-foot coordination and hand-eye coordination.

### OBJECT
To score points by running around the bases.

### EQUIPMENT
Kickball and kickball court.

## PROCEDURE

1) One child is chosen to be the first kicker. Another is chosen to be the pitcher. Everyone else who wants to be in the game goes in the outfield.

2) The pitcher, in the center of the court, rolls the ball to the kicker who is at one of the corners of the court designated "Home Plate". The kicker kicks the ball as far as possible into the field. He takes off in all possible haste and runs the bases (the 3 other corners of the court) in succession in a counter clockwise direction.

3) The kicker must touch every base and shout "Home Run!" as he crosses home plate. He should not stop on any base.

4) The person in the field who catches the ball runs as quickly as possible to the pitcher's plate. When he touches it, he must shout "Out!" before the runner shouts "Home Run!", at which time the fielder becomes the next kicker and the kicker becomes the pitcher.

5) If the kicker makes a home run, he is up again. The fielder goes back out to try again. Only the person who actually caught the ball may put the runner out. He may not throw it to anyone else. A caught fly ball is an automatic out.

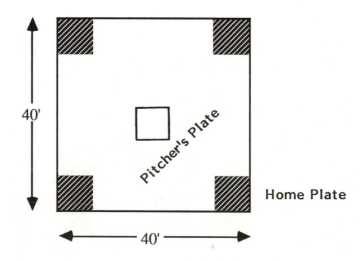

# HOP SCOTCH

### GOOD FOR
Hand-eye coordination and sequencing of numbers 1-10.

### OBJECT
To successfully execute both throwing and hopping skills in order from 1-10.

### EQUIPMENT
Lager (marker) and Hop Scotch court.

## PROCEDURE

1)  First child throws her marker into box #1.

2)  She hops to the end of the court and out, turns around and hops back. She may not hop in any box that has a marker.

3)  When she returns to the square next in sequence to the one with her marker, she stays on one foot and without putting her other foot down or using her extra hand for support, picks up her marker.

4)  She then hops into box one where her marker was and hops out of the court. If she has completed the first box without any misses (fouls), she then proceeds to box #2 and so forth until a miss (foul) occurs.

5)  Children take turns, always starting where they left off, until someone has completed every box. When a child fouls, she may place her marker in the correct box to be there for her next turn.

## Fouls:

1)  Losing balance while picking up a marker or using hands to support oneself while picking up a marker.

2)  Failing to throw a marker entirely into the correct box.

3)  Hopping into a box that contains a marker.

4)  Stepping on a line.

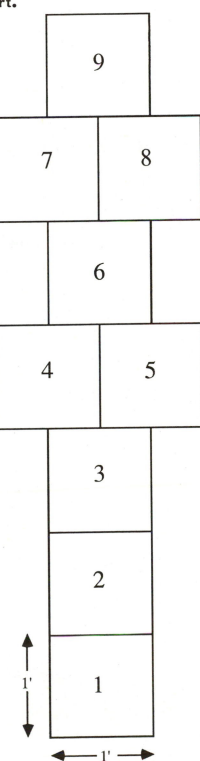

# HORIZONTAL LADDER

### GOOD FOR
Upper arm strength.

### OBJECT
To cross ladder in an alternating hand pattern.

### EQUIPMENT
Horizontal ladder over protective surface.

## PROCEDURE

1)    All students start from the same end of the ladder.

2)    Students use two hands at all times.

3)    Students should never sit or pull head above the bars on the horizontal ladder.

### Safety Consideration

Equipment over four feet high should have a six foot protective surface on all sides of the equipment.

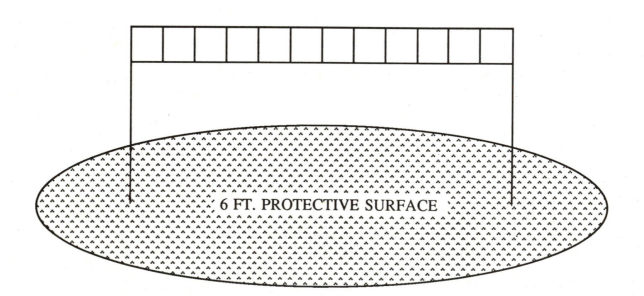

6 FT. PROTECTIVE SURFACE

# NATIONBALL

### GOOD FOR
Hand-eye coordination, body and space awareness and locomotor practice.

### OBJECT
To keep from being hit by the ball so that you and your teammates
are the only ones left.

### EQUIPMENT
Utility ball or basketball and a rectangular court.

PROCEDURE

1) Two teams, which may consist of any number of players, occupy their respective halves of the field.

2) Each team selects a temporary goalie. The temporary goalie becomes a regular player when one player of his team has been hit by the ball.

3) Actual play is started by a jump ball.

4) Each team's goalies are behind the end lines on the side of the opposing teams.

5) Players must keep at least one foot in their respective playing areas.

6) Goalies may retrieve a ball beyond the side lines but may not cross the center line or enter the team playing areas.

7) Goalie must have one foot behind the endline in order to be eligible to shoot or throw the ball at the opposing player. The goalie may pass the ball to their team players or other goalies along their end line.

8) After being hit with a ball from an opposing team player or goalie, the player becomes a goalie for his team.

9) A ball caught without touching the ground is not counted a hit and may be shot or passed.

10) If a player is hit by one's own teammate or goalie, it does not count.

11) Only the first person hit counts.

12) Hits above the waist do not count.

13) Ball thrown to hit above the shoulders is grounds for disqualification.

14) Players can not pick up the ball, only the goalies can when it rolls outside of the court.

15) Players may not step over the center line.

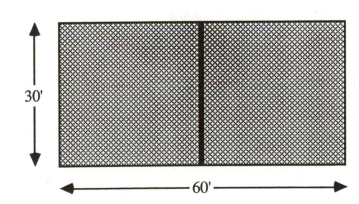

# PICKLE

### GOOD FOR
Hand-eye coordination.

### OBJECT
To score points by successully running from one base to another without getting tagged.

### EQUIPMENT
A ball and two bases.


PROCEDURE

1)   Two players are basemen and another player is the runner.

2)   The basemen throw the ball back and  forth between them.  The runner tries to time his running with the throwing so that he may run between bases without being tagged by a baseman with the ball.

3)   The runner scores a point every time he can tag a base while the ball is being thrown.  If he is tagged by a baseman, he is out and goes to the end of the wait line.  (Tagging is done by a baseman touching the runner with the ball while the ball is held securely by the baseman.)  The baseman tagging the runner becomes the new runner and a new player comes in to replace the baseman.

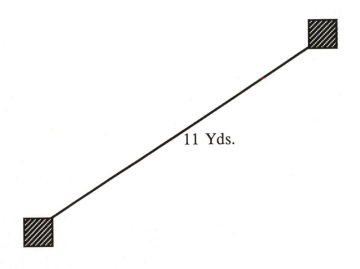

11 Yds.

# PRISONER

## GOOD FOR
Hand-eye coordination and cooperative learning.

## OBJECT
To eliminate opponents by throwing the ball over the net into the opponent's court.
If ball bounces, then the person who's name was called is eliminated
and becomes a "prisoner".

## EQUIPMENT
Volleyball and volleyball court with net.

PROCEDURE

1) The class is divided into two teams. Each occupying one half of a volleyball court.

2) The game begins when a player tosses the ball over the net and calls out a name of someone on the opposing team. If the ball is caught, then the game continues (receiving team throws, etc.). If the ball is not caught, then the person whose name was called becomes a "prisoner" and the prisoner's team now throws the ball.

3) To free a prisoner, it is necessary for the thrower on the team throwing the ball to call "prisoner" and if the ball is missed then the prisoner is freed. If however, the ball is caught, then the prisoner must remain in jail and it's the receiving team's turn to throw the ball to the other team.

4) The game continues until one team has a jail full of prisoners. In that case, the other team would win.

5) On every throw a player must call either a name or prisoner. If this is forgotten, then the thrower must go to jail.

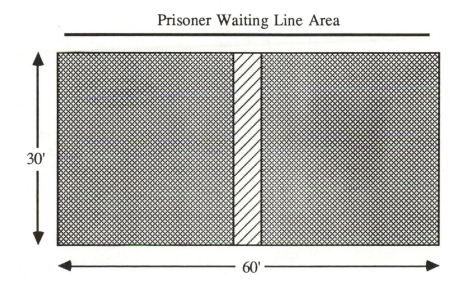

Prisoner Waiting Line Area

30'

60'

# RATTLE SNAKE

### GOOD FOR
Eye-foot coordination and jumping skills.

### OBJECT
To remain an "active" player by successfully jumping over the rope.

### EQUIPMENT
Long rope.

PROCEDURE

1) Two children hold the ends of the rope as in "skip rope".

2) They squat down and wiggle the rope back and fourth on the ground as vigorously as possible. The other children line up behind a leader on one side of the rope. They try, one at a time, to run and jump over without touching the rattle snake.

3) The leader goes all of the way around to the end of the line after her jump to keep all the running and jumping action going in the same direction.

4) Anyone who touches the rope must take a rope end and the rope holder joins the jumpers.

-----------------------------------------------------------------------

# BASIC ROPE SKIPPING CHALLENGES

### GOOD FOR
Eye-foot coordination and cardiovascular fitness.

### OBJECT
To successfully complete basic jump rope stunts 1-14.

### EQUIPMENT
Short jump ropes: K-3 grades = 7 ft ropes; 4-5 grades = 8 ft ropes;
6-9 grades = 9 ft ropes;  and 9-12 grades = 10 ft ropes.

PROCEDURE

The following two pages of descriptions and illustrations were provided by, and with the permission of, the American Heart Association.  Jump rope videos, instructional manuals, and handouts are provided by the AMA through their Jump Rope For Heart national campaigns.  For more information, please call your local Heart Association office or the AMA National Headquarters at 1-800-527-6941.

## 1. Side Swing
1. Twirl rope to one side
2. Repeat on the opposite side
3. Twirl rope alternately from side to side

Teaching Hints: Keep hands together, keep feet together.

## 2. Basic Jump (single bounce)
1. Jump on both feet
2. Land on balls of feet

Teaching Hints: Keep feet, ankles and knees together.

## 3. Double side swing and jump
1. Twirl rope to left side
2. Twirl rope to right side
3. Jump over rope

Teaching Hints: Keep hands together on side swings, keep feet together.

## 4. Single side swing and jump
1. Twirl rope to left side    3. Twirl rope to right side
2. Jump over rope    4. Jump over rope

Teaching Hints: Keep hands together on side swings, keep feet together.

## 5. Skier (side to side)
1. Jump left
2. Jump right

Teaching Hints: Feet move laterally 4-6″ to each side, keep feet together.

## 6. Bell (forward and backward)
1. Jump forward
2. Jump backward

Teaching Hints: Feet move 4-6″ forward & backward as a bell clapper, keep feet together.

## 7. Straddle (spread together)
1. Jump to a straddle position
2. Return to basic bounce

Teaching Hints: Spread feet shoulder width apart.

## 8. Scissors
1. Jump to stride position with left foot forward
2. Jump and reverse position of feet

Teaching Hints: Feet 8-12″ apart.

1.    2.

## 9. Straddle Cross
1. Jump to straddle position
2. Jump to crossed legs

Teaching Hints: Feet shoulder width apart.

1.    2.

## 10. Wounded duck (alternate toes/heels together)
1. Jump, toes & knees touch, heels spread
2. Jump, heels touch, toes and knees spread

Teaching Hints: Alternate toes touching and heels touching.

1.    2.

## 11. Crossover (cross arms)
1. Cross arms and jump
2. Open rope, basic bounce

Teaching Hints: Cross right arm over left, cross left arm over right.

1.    2.

## 12. Full turn (one complete circle with rope in front)
1. Turn body left, with right turn of rope
2. Side swing right, body turns right
3. Full turn body makes full turn to right
4. Jump rope forward

Teaching Hints: Follow rope, rope and body may turn left.

1.    2.    3.    4.

## 13. Heel to Heel
1. Jump and touch left heel
2. Jump and touch right heel

Teaching Hints: Heel touches are forward.

1.    2.

## 14. Toe to toe (alternate toe touch)
1. Hops on left foot, touch right toe
2. Hops on right foot, touch left toe

Teaching Hints: Keep body over weighted foot.

1.    2.

# ADVANCED ROPE SKIPPING CHALLENGES

### GOOD FOR
Hand-eye coordination.

### OBJECT
To successfully execute skills in order listed below.

### EQUIPMENT
Long rope, short rope, and a ball.

PROCEDURE

1)    Child jumps in rope turned by two friends.  At the same time he bounces a ball.

2)    Child jumps in short individual rope while jumping in the long rope.

3)    Two children jump inside a large rope while playing catch with one another.

4)    One child jumps inside a long rope while playing catch with someone outside of the rope.

5)    Four children turn two long ropes with one of the ropes at a right angle to the other while one child on the end of the right angled rope nearest the middle of the other rope jumps into the center of that rope.

6)    Have the children invent their own tricks.

-------------------------------------------------------------------

# SIXTEEN EXERCISES

### GOOD FOR
Fitness activity.

### OBJECT
Execute exercises in boxes 1-16, in order, without stopping.

### EQUIPMENT
Sixteen square court (see diagram on page 29 ).

PROCEDURE

Any series of sixteen exercises can be taught during P.E. time and performed in sequence around the court.  The children memorize the sequence, that is, do one toe touch in box one, two push ups in box two, three jumping jacks in box three, four sit-ups in box four.....sixteen jumps in box sixteen.  Children try to complete the course before the end of recess or see how many times they can do it.  Many students may work at once.

# SIXTEEN SQUARE

**GOOD FOR**
Hand-eye coordination.

**OBJECT**
To get to and remain in, box #1.

**EQUIPMENT**
Playground ball and Sixteen Square court (see diagram on page 29).

PROCEDURE

1) The game is the same as Four Square except that the leader (and server) is in box #1 and waiting players are outside of box #16. Players try to work their way up to box #1.

2) In Sixteen Square, the court is divided into 4 Sections which play against each other. For example, Section A, which always serves (child in box #1 of Section A is always the server), consists of boxes 1, 2, 7 & 8; Section B = boxes 3, 4, 5 & 6; Section C = boxes 11, 12, 13 & 14; and Section D = boxes 9, 10, 15 & 16. Within each Section a child occupies a box and is responsible for hitting the ball from their box in their Section. When a child misses the ball or otherwise fouls out, she goes to the waiting line outside of box #16 and everyone on box numbers below her move up one number (of course, this assumes the logic that box #1 is the highest and box #16 is the lowest, or to put it in terms of the box numbers' numerical value, everyone on larger box numbers move down one number). The top position in each Section is the upper left-hand box (Section A = box #1, Section B = box #3, Section C = box #11 and Section D = box #9) and the lowest position in each Section is the lower left-hand box (Section A = box #8, Section B = box #6, Section C = box #14 and Section D = box #16).

3) Naturally, it would be better to have four games of Four Square going, which you can certainly do if you have enough balls. But it often happens that each class of thirty children has only one ball, so this game is tailor-made for the "one ball" situation. If twenty children want to play Four Square around a regular Four Square game, sixteen of them have to wait in line and it takes a long time to get into the game. However, when sixteen of the children are in the game, only four students are not actively involved.

4) Because of the dynamics of Sixteen Square, children get into the game very quickly and are more likely to become actively involved.

5) Another version of Sixteen Square is instead of having each child who is out being replaced by the child in the box below them, replace each Section that has an out no matter what child in that Section is at fault. (Serving Section would rotate the serve among themselves.) This game will really move with four children coming in and going out at a time!

| 1 | 2 | 3 | 4 |
| 8 | 7 | 6 | 5 |
| 9 | 10 | 11 | 12 |
| 16 | 15 | 14 | 13 |

4'

4'

-----------------------------------------------------------------

# SLIDES

### GOOD FOR
Balance.

### OBJECT
To climb slide, slide down, and land on feet.

### EQUIPMENT
Slide.

## PROCEDURE

Students always climb ladder to get to the top.  Students should use both hands at all times.  Students climb one step at a time.  Students always slide down feet first.  And, students wait until previous child is off the slide.

## Safety Considerations

A six foot protective surface should be on all sides of the slide.  Slides are oriented in a northerly direction to avoid heat build up on sliding surfaces.  And a primary grade school slide should not exceed ten feet.

# MODIFIED SOCCER

### GOOD FOR
Eye-foot coordination.

### OBJECT
To score points by kicking the ball through the goal box.

### EQUIPMENT
Soccer ball and an all purpose field (see diagram and note that goal box
should be about 12 ft long and 6 ft wide).

## PROCEDURE

1) Game begins with a kick-off.  A kick-off also occurs after each goal made.

2) Six minute running time quarters are recommended for elementary age students.

3) When the ball goes out-of-bounds it is put into play by the opposing team with a throw in.

4) Attacking players must be even with, or behind, the line of the ball.

## Fouls:

1) Personal fouls include unnecessary roughness, tripping, striking, charging, holding, and pushing.  This results in a free kick for the other team.

2) It is also a foul for any player, except the goalkeeper, to handle the ball with the arms or hands.  Result---free kick for opponents.

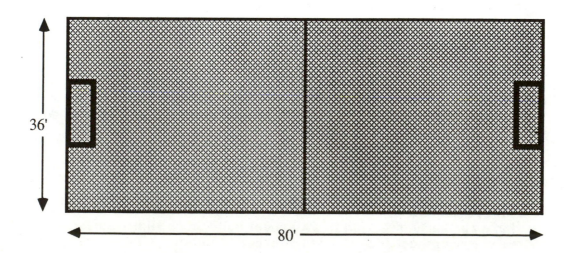

# SWINGS

**GOOD FOR**
Vestibular stimulation.

**OBJECT**
To swing unassisted by executing correct pumping motion.

**EQUIPMENT**
Swings.

PROCEDURE

1) You may swing until the person waiting counts to 20.

2) Swing forward and backwards only.

3) Bring the swing to a stop and step off.  No jumping!

4) Only one person may swing on a swing at a time.

5) Hold on with both hands at all times.

6) Empty swings should not be pushed or twisted.

Safety Considerations

1) A protective surface 7 ft wide should be on all sides of the swinging area.

2) The swings should be enclosed by a box so that other children do not wander into the swing's path.

----------------------------------------------------------------------

# TETHER BALL

**GOOD FOR**
Hand-eye coordination.

**OBJECT**
To wrap rope completely around the pole and thereby eliminating opponent.

**EQUIPMENT**
Tether ball and pole in middle of 10 ft diameter court.

PROCEDURE

1) Players stand on opposite sides of the circle.  They may not step into opponent's side of the court.

2) In order to achieve the object of the game, players need to wind the cord in the desired direction by hitting the ball with one or both hands, opened or closed.

3)    The opponent tries to hit, and thus wind, the approaching ball in the opposite direction.

4)    To start the game, the server can stand anywhere on his side of the court to strike the ball.

Fouls:

(The penalty for a foul is the loss of the game.)

1)    Hitting the ball with any part of the body other than the hands.

2)    Catching or holding the ball during play.

3)    Touching the pole.

4)    Touching the rope.

5)    Throwing the ball.

6)    Stepping on the outer or inner boundaries.

7)    Double hits.

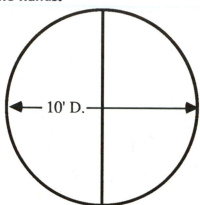

--------------------------------------------------------------------

# TOUCH FOOTBALL

### GOOD FOR
Hand-eye coordination and locomotor practice.

### OBJECT
To score points by crossing the opponents' goal line with
either a caught pass or by running the football.

### EQUIPMENT
Football and rectangular playing field.

### PROCEDURE

1)    The game is started with a kick-off.  The loser of the coin toss kicks-off to the opposing team from their goal line.

2)    If the kick-off is kicked out of bounds, take it over.

3)    The kick-off may not be recovered by the kicking team unless caught and then fumbled by the receivers.

4)    A team has four downs (four consecutive plays) to score or they lose the ball.

5)    A team in possession of the ball has 30 seconds to huddle and play their play.

6)    Blocking is done with arms close to the body.

7)    A player is down when an opposing player touches them with two hands.  (Flags may be used here.)

8) A ball carrier must make an attempt to avoid the defensive player and is not permitted to run over or through the defensive player.

9) All forward passes must be thrown from behind the line of scrimmage. (Line of scrimmage is the point from which the ball was hiked.)

10) All players on the field are eligible to receive and intercept passes.

11) All fumbles are dead at the spot of the fumble.

12) All punts must be announced. Neither team may cross the line of scrimmage until the ball is kicked.

13) A touchdown is a pass caught or carried into the end zone. This scores six points. A completed pass or run after a touchdown on the subsequent play is worth two and one point respectively.

**Penalties Resulting In 5 Yard Loss:**

1) Being offsides.

2) Delay of game.

3) Passing from a spot in front of the line of scrimmage.

4) Ball carrier not avoiding a defensive player.

5) Failure to announce punt.

**Penalties Resulting in 15 Yard Loss:**

1) Holding, illegal tackling.

2) Illegal blocking (from behind).

3) Unsportsmanlike conduct.

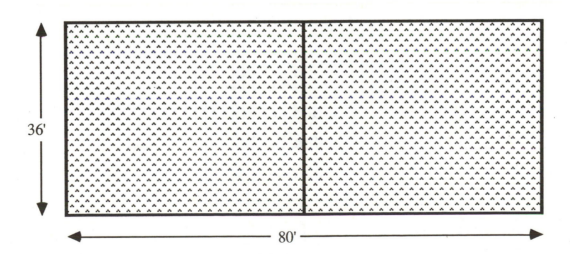

36'

80'

# TWENTY ONE

## GOOD FOR
Hand-eye coordination.

## OBJECT
To score 21 points by shooting the ball into the basket.

## EQUIPMENT
Basketball, basket and a 15 ft square court.

PROCEDURE

1)   Players line up behind the court foul line at the side opposite the basket.  The first player shoots as many baskets as she can without missing.  She scores two points for each basket.

2)   When she misses, she must catch the ball before it bounces twice and shoot from the spot where she catches it.

3)   If she scores, she gets one point.  Whether she scores or not, the next child takes her turn.

4)   The first child to score 21 points is the winner.  Children accumulate points with each turn and must remember their score as the game progresses.

5)   Winner must score exactly 21 points.  If she scores 22, she must start all over again to score exactly 21.  As she starts over, she is automatically given one point to build on.

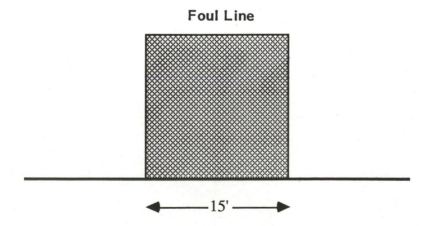

Foul Line

←——— 15' ———→

# VOLLEYBALL

### GOOD FOR
Hand-eye coordination.

### OBJECT
To score points by serving and returning the ball over the net
so that opponents are unable to return it.

### EQUIPMENT
Volleyball and volleyball court with net.

## PROCEDURE

1)    A volleyball team consists of six players.

2)    Play begins with the serve.  Only the serving team can score by their opponents' failure to hit (return) the ball back.  The server retains the serve, scoring consecutive points until his side fails to make a good return.

3)    "Side Out" results when the serving team fails to serve the ball successfully or fails to make a good return.

4)    Members of each team take turns serving in sequence.

5)    All lines are considered as part of the court and therefore are "in".

6)    Game is played to 15 points.  A team must win by 2 points.


Violations:

1)    Touching the net.

2)    Holding the ball.

3)    Stepping over the center line.

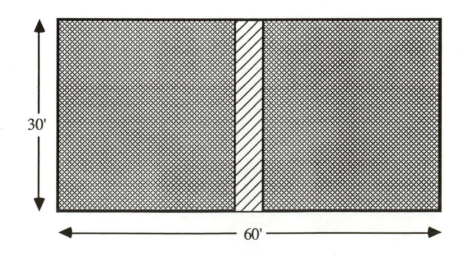

APPENDIX – 1

# AWARDS

The Playground Good Sport Coupons can be used by teacher and playground supervisors to acknowledge appropriate behavior by students. This type of a positive reward system is based on a "catch them being good" philosophy. Coupons can be earned towards a monthly Good Sport Award. (See examples of each on the following two pages and feel free to make as many copies as you need.)

**good sport coupon**

name

date

room

grade

signed

**good sport coupon**

name

date

room

grade

signed

**good sport coupon**

name

date

room

grade

signed

**good sport coupon**

name

date

room

grade

signed

# PLAYGROUND

## "Good Sport Award"

Presented to _____

on this _____ day of _____ ,19 _____ .

signed _____
Principal

## APPENDIX - 2

# SAFETY AND LAWSUITS

Eighty percent of all school related accidents occur during recess, lunch and physical education. For this reason, coupled with the recent number of lawsuits dealing with injuries that occur in school, it makes good sense to devise school-wide playground rules and procedures to follow for safety awareness.

In establishing school site safety rules it may be of benefit to understand that in a lawsuit the injured party must prove negligence. The four elements of negligence include:

1)    duty of care existed and was owed to the person injured

2)    duty of care was breached

3)    injury was a result of the breach of duty of care

4)    damage did occur


Below you will find a list of the nine factors commonly cited in attempts to prove negligence:

1)    use of unqualified personnel

2)    inadequate supervision

3)    inadequately prepared P.E. instructor

4)    inadequate or improper instructor

5)    improper conditioning or training

6)    unsafe areas or facilities for P.E. instruction

7)    unenforced safety rules or regulations

8)    defective defensive equipment

9)    improper treatment of injuries


## NOTE

The information for Appendix-2 was adapted from P.E. Playground And Field Safety For Grades K-12, written by Bonnie Mohnsen. For a more complete accounting of P.E. Safety and Lawsuits write for her book available from: The Los Angeles County Schools Publications Department, Office of the Los Angeles County Superintendent of Schools, 9300 E. Imperial Hwy, Downey, California 90242. (Phone: 213-922-6111)

## SUPERVISION CHECKLIST

Supervision is by far the most critical element in negligence lawsuits.

( )   Supervisors follow written rules and guidelines consistent with school-wide safety procedures.

( )   Supervision is spaced throughout the playground.

( )   Ratios of students to supervisors should never exceed 50 to 1.

( )   Supervisors arrive promptly and stay alert to dangerous play.

( )   Playground is inspected daily for safety considerations.

## STUDENT INJURIES PROCEDURE CHECKLIST

( )   Emergency procedures are in writing and distributed to the staff.

( )   School maintains current emergency cards on each student.

( )   Supervisors use sound judgement in the event of an injury. Whenever possible, send for the administrator and school nurse.

( )   Parents are contacted immediately.

( )   Emergency drills are practiced monthly.

( )   Accident reports completed and filed.

( )   Each accident should be investigated and reviewed for further safety considerations.

APPENDIX - 3

# EQUIPMENT RECOMMENDATIONS

Below are listed equipment items needed for a peaceful playground program as described in this book. For optimal results in your own program, use specific equipment sizes and quantities when specified (based on 400 students).

| Equipment Item | Quantity Needed | Size Specified (if any) |
|---|---|---|
| utility balls | 15 | 8 ½" |
| basketballs | 4 | |
| bean bags | 24 | |
| scoops | 12 | |
| chinese ropes | 6 | |
| popsicle sticks | 12 | |
| kickballs | 4 | |
| softballs (nerf) | 4 | |
| volleyballs | 4 | |
| long jump ropes | 6 | 16-20 ft |
| short jump ropes | 24 | 7-8 ft |
| soccer balls | 4 | |
| tether balls | 6 | |
| footballs | 6 | |

# Equipment Check-Out Sheet

Date_____ Recess _____ Teacher_____

| Name | Room # | Equipment Out | In |
|------|--------|---------------|-----|
|  |  |  |  |
|  |  |  |  |
|  |  |  |  |
|  |  |  |  |
|  |  |  |  |
|  |  |  |  |
|  |  |  |  |
|  |  |  |  |
|  |  |  |  |
|  |  |  |  |
|  |  |  |  |
|  |  |  |  |
|  |  |  |  |

APPENDIX – 4

# GAMES AND FIELD MARKINGS

This section is included for easy reference. Some of the markings have been included in earlier game suggestions. Note that additional activity diagrams such as the Number and Alpha Bet Grids, Scattered Circles, Midline Jumping, Cross-Over Walking and Skipping, and Alpha Bet Tracks have been added due to their developmental value and skill acquisition.

Basic Grass Court 80 ft x 36 ft

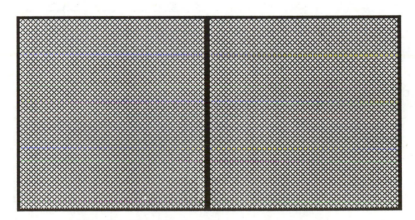

Basic Blacktop Court 60 ft x 30 ft

| 6 | 4 | 7 |
|---|---|---|
| 2 | 12 | 3 |
| 11 | 5 | 8 |
| 9 | 1 | 10 |

1.5'

1.5'

**Number Grid**

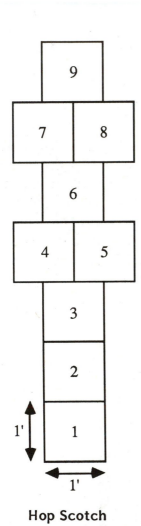

**Hop Scotch**

| I | M | N | G | S | P |
|---|---|---|---|---|---|
| W | E | B | O | A | U |
| Q | A | U | I | R | D |
| J | F | O | T | E | V |
| Z | E | S | C | A | K |
| L | Y | H | R | M | X |

1'

1'

**Alphabet Grid**

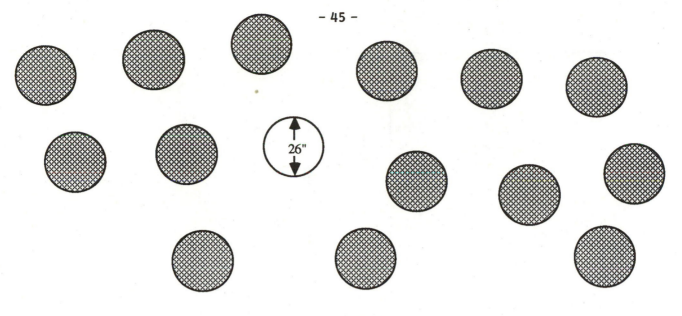

Scattered Circles

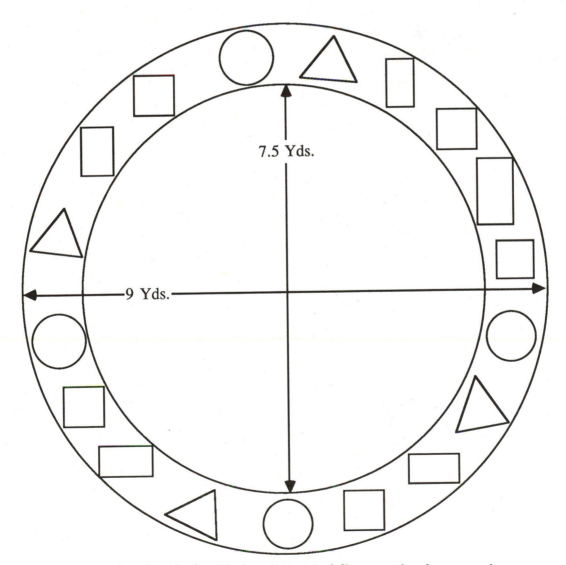

7.5 Yds.

9 Yds.

Multi Use Circle for kindergarten and first grade playgrounds.

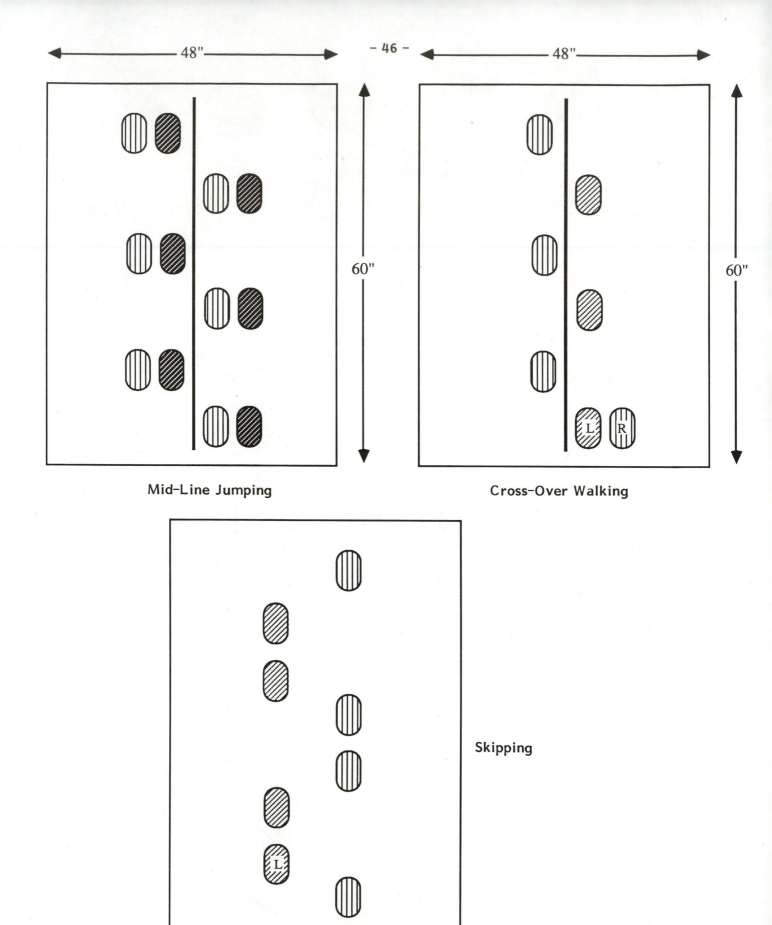

48"

60"

**Mid-Line Jumping**

48"

60"

**Cross-Over Walking**

**Skipping**

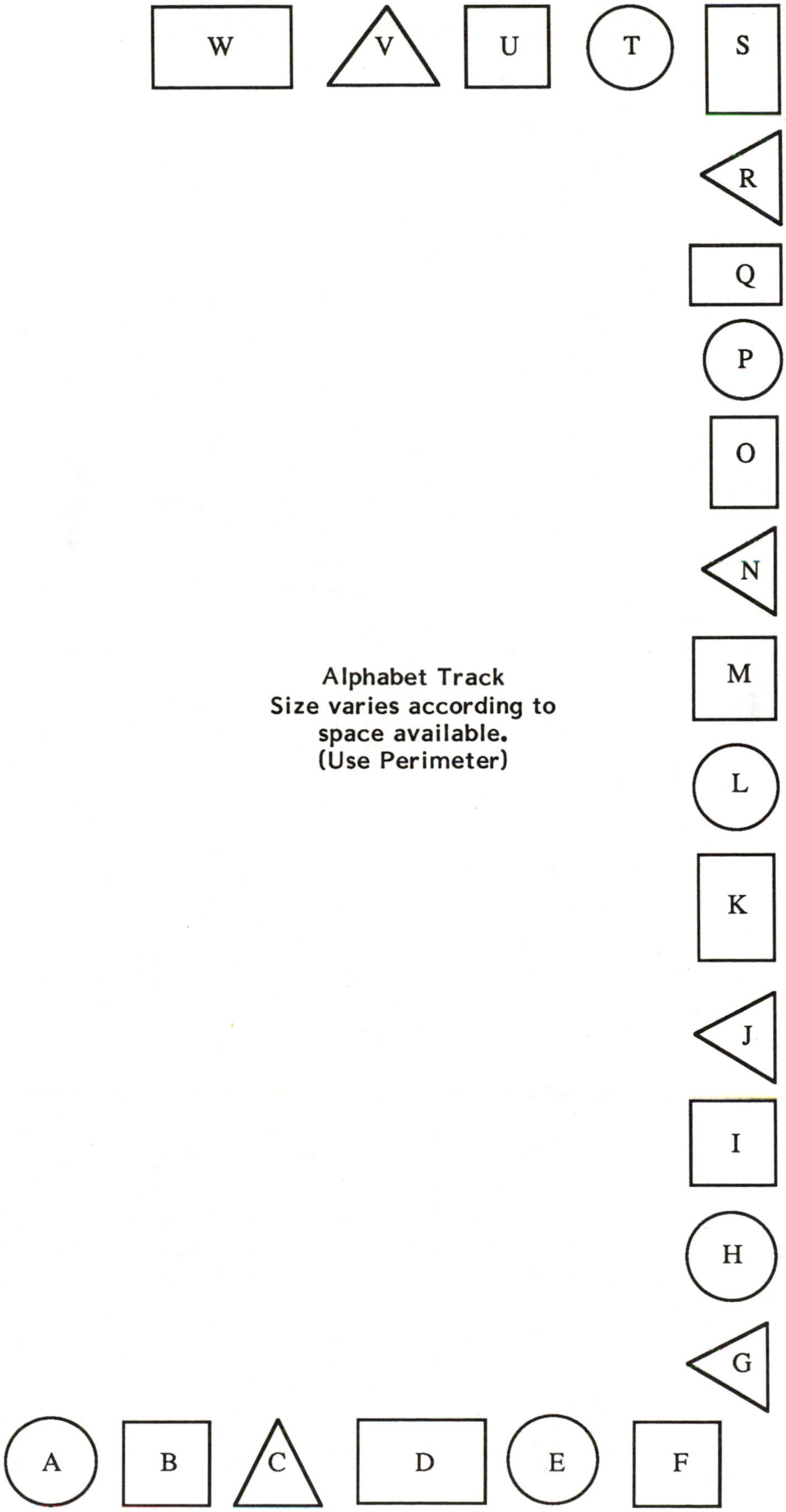

W V U T S

R

Q

P

O

N

M

Alphabet Track
Size varies according to
space available.
(Use Perimeter)

L

K

J

I

H

G

A B C D E F

Elementary School 220 Yard Track

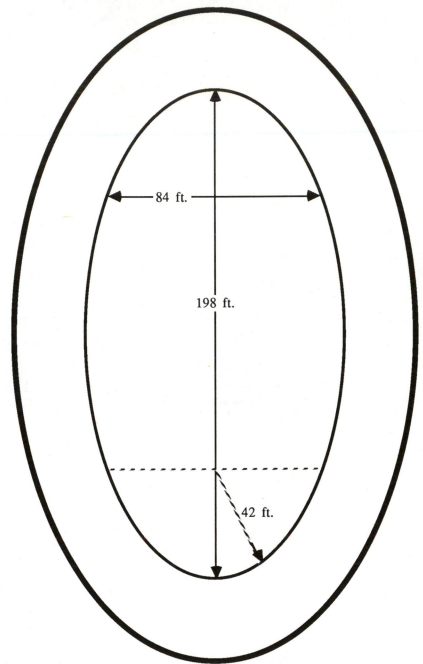

Most elementary schools have neither the space or the funds for a 440 yard track facility. A 220 yard track, however, can be economically burned into an elementary school playground and requires a minimum amount of space while allowing for tremendous fitness payoffs.

<u>Key</u>

2 laps = ¼ mile

4 laps = ½ mile

8 laps = one mile

# REFERENCES

American Heart Association (1983) <u>Jump For The Heart Of It (Basic Skills)</u>

Austin, Barbara (1977) <u>Peace On The Playground</u> handout, Elementary P.E. Workshop, Cal Poly, California

Dauer and Pangrazzi (1986) <u>Dynamic Physical Education For Elementary School Children</u> 8th Edition

Los Angeles County Schools Office, California, <u>Playground And Field Markings For Elementary Schools</u>

Mohnsen, Bonnie <u>P.E. Playground And Field Safety For Grades K-12</u> Distributed by the Los Angeles County Office Of Education, California

-------------------------------------------------------------------

## ! WORKSHOPS & CONSULTATION !

Contact the author directly for information concerning workshops and consultation in "Peaceful Playgrounds" for your situation.

Write:

Melinda Bossenmeyer
2097 Ontario Ave
Corona, California 91720

Or Call: 714-737-7105

-------------------------------------------------------------------

## ! FREE PUBLISHER'S CATALOG !

Send for a FREE catalog of

INNOVATIVE CURRICULUM GUIDEBOOKS AND MATERIALS

in

Movement Education, Special Education and Perceptual-Motor Development

Write:

FRONT ROW EXPERIENCE
540 Discovery Bay Blvd.
Byron, California 94514

Questions?  Call 415-634-5710

# YOUR MARKINGS